The just man walketh in his integrity: his children are blessed after him.

Proverbs 20:7

The just man walketh in his integrity: his children are blessed after him.

Proverbs 20:7

The just man walketh in his integrity: his children are blessed after him.

Proverbs 20:7

The just man walketh in his integrity: his children are blessed after him.

Proverbs 20:7

The just man walketh in his integrity: his children are blessed after him.

Proverbs 20:7

The just man walketh in his integrity: his children are blessed after him.

Proverbs 20:7

The just man walketh in his integrity: his children are blessed after him.

Proverbs 20:7

The just man walketh in his integrity: his children are blessed after him.

Proverbs 20:7

The just man walketh in his integrity: his children are blessed after him.

Proverbs 20:7

The just man walketh in his integrity: his children are blessed after him.

Proverbs 20:7

The just man walketh in his integrity: his children are blessed after him.

Proverbs 20:7

The just man walketh in his integrity: his children are blessed after him.

Proverbs 20:7

The just man walketh in his integrity: his children are blessed after him.

Proverbs 20:7

The just man walketh in his integrity: his children are blessed after him.

Proverbs 20:7

The just man walketh in his integrity: his children are blessed after him.

Proverbs 20:7

The just man walketh in his integrity: his children are blessed after him.

Proverbs 20:7

The just man walketh in his integrity: his children are blessed after him.

Proverbs 20:7

The just man walketh in his integrity: his children are blessed after him.

Proverbs 20:7

The just man walketh in his integrity: his children are blessed after him.

Proverbs 20:7

The just man walketh in his integrity: his children are blessed after him.

Proverbs 20:7

The just man walketh in his integrity: his children are blessed after him.

Proverbs 20:7

The just man walketh in his integrity: his children are blessed after him.

Proverbs 20:7

The just man walketh in his integrity: his children are blessed after him.

Proverbs 20:7

The just man walketh in his integrity: his children are blessed after him.

Proverbs 20:7

> The just man walketh in his integrity: his children are blessed after him.
>
> Proverbs 20:7

The just man walketh in his integrity: his children are blessed after him.

Proverbs 20:7

The just man walketh in his integrity: his children are blessed after him.

Proverbs 20:7

The just man walketh in his integrity: his children are blessed after him.

Proverbs 20:7

The just man walketh in his integrity: his children are blessed after him.

Proverbs 20:7

The just man walketh in his integrity: his children are blessed after him.

Proverbs 20:7

The just man walketh in his integrity: his children are blessed after him.

Proverbs 20:7

The just man walketh in his integrity: his children are blessed after him.

Proverbs 20:7

The just man walketh in his integrity: his children are blessed after him.

Proverbs 20:7

The just man walketh in his integrity: his children are blessed after him.

Proverbs 20:7

The just man walketh in his integrity: his children are blessed after him.

Proverbs 20:7

The just man walketh in his integrity: his children are blessed after him.

Proverbs 20:7

The just man walketh in his integrity: his children are blessed after him.

Proverbs 20:7

The just man walketh in his integrity: his children are blessed after him.

Proverbs 20:7

> The just man walketh in his integrity: his children are blessed after him.
>
> Proverbs 20:7

The just man walketh in his integrity: his children are blessed after him.

Proverbs 20:7

The just man walketh in his integrity: his children are blessed after him.

Proverbs 20:7

The just man walketh in his integrity: his children are blessed after him.

Proverbs 20:7

The just man walketh in his integrity: his children are blessed after him.

Proverbs 20:7

The just man walketh in his integrity: his children are blessed after him.

Proverbs 20:7

The just man walketh in his integrity: his children are blessed after him.

Proverbs 20:7

The just man walketh in his integrity: his children are blessed after him.

Proverbs 20:7

The just man walketh in his integrity: his children are blessed after him.

Proverbs 20:7

The just man walketh in his integrity: his children are blessed after him.

Proverbs 20:7

The just man walketh in his integrity: his children are blessed after him.

Proverbs 20:7

The just man walketh in his integrity: his children are blessed after him.

Proverbs 20:7

The just man walketh in his integrity: his children are blessed after him.

Proverbs 20:7

The just man walketh in his integrity: his children are blessed after him.

Proverbs 20:7

The just man walketh in his integrity: his children are blessed after him.

Proverbs 20:7

The just man walketh in his integrity: his children are blessed after him.

Proverbs 20:7

The just man walketh in his integrity: his children are blessed after him.

Proverbs 20:7

The just man walketh in his integrity: his children are blessed after him.

Proverbs 20:7

The just man walketh in his integrity: his children are blessed after him.

Proverbs 20:7

The just man walketh in his integrity: his children are blessed after him.

Proverbs 20:7

The just man walketh in his integrity: his children are blessed after him.

Proverbs 20:7

The just man walketh in his integrity: his children are blessed after him.

Proverbs 20:7

The just man walketh in his integrity: his children are blessed after him.

Proverbs 20:7

The just man walketh in his integrity: his children are blessed after him.

Proverbs 20:7

The just man walketh in his integrity: his children are blessed after him.

Proverbs 20:7

The just man walketh in his integrity: his children are blessed after him.

Proverbs 20:7

> The just man walketh in his integrity: his children are blessed after him.
>
> Proverbs 20:7